GETTING INTO

Art & Design

THIRD EDITION

TROTMAN

Getting into Art & Design
This third edition, revised by John Parker and Nick Fogg,
published in 2000
by Trotman & Company Ltd
2 The Green, Richmond, Surrey TW9 1PL

© Trotman and Company Limited 2000

British Library Cataloguing in Publication Data
A catalogue record for this book is available from the
British Library

ISBN 0 85660 546 8

Typeset by Florence Production Ltd, Stoodleigh, Devon
Printed and bound in Great Britain
Creative Print & Design (Wales) Ltd

The Trotman Web Site

The Trotman Publishing Web Site has been developed for all those interested in careers and higher education.

Each address has its own distinct function, and all are accessible from the Trotman Publishing home page (www.trotmanpublishing.co.uk).
Bookmark these sites and benefit from using our online services.

www.trotmanpublishing.co.uk
All our company information at the click of a mouse button

- Publication dates – know what is coming and when
- Read reviews of books – what other people have said about them
- *Win Your Rent* online entry
- Contact us – give us your feedback
- Special offers – take advantage of seasonal offers

www.careers-portal.co.uk
A links portal site dedicated to careers guidance

- 1,700 links in an easy-to-use search format
- Use the search facility to locate sites by subject
- Voted by The Daily Mail one of the Top Ten careers sites

www.careersuk.co.uk
The UK's only online e-commerce bookstore dedicated to careers

- Over 300 careers-related book and CD-ROM titles
- Fast database interrogation allows searches by title, author, subject or ISBN
- Order directly over the internet using our secure credit card facility

So whatever you want to know about careers resources, news or organisations, it's available online from
Trotman

CONTENTS

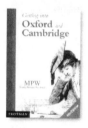

PREFACE

We live in a world of constant and rapid change, driven by global economic pressures and the need for organisations, companies, countries and individuals to be competitive.

The world of work has mirrored these changes – old industries and careers have disappeared seemingly overnight, while new sectors, many requiring flexible and transferable creative skills, have emerged.

The world of art and design has also experienced other great changes, coping with rapid developments in technology and communications. Ever-creative and adaptive, the design industry has ridden this second industrial revolution to emerge as a strong, vibrant and major industrial sector both in the UK and on a global scale.

The British design and creative services sectors have a worldwide reputation for innovation and excellence, which reflects our attention to both formal design education and the sheer breadth of commercial creative activity taking place in our economy, ranging from traditional crafts to cutting-edge computer-based design.

This period of exciting and seemingly sustainable growth has opened up greater opportunities for young people to build a career path in the creative industries. Art and design has always been a competitive marketplace for employment but never before has there been such a great choice of training options and job roles.

This book sets out to guide you through the main career options available and some of the routes you may take to get there. It is a step on the way towards an exciting career!

'Culture and creativity are vital to our national life. Creative people enrich us all by the exercise of their imagination. They produce many of the things that make life worth living. But there is another reason for cherishing creativity . . . in the United Kingdom, the creative industries generate revenues approaching £60 billion a year. They contribute over 4 per cent to the domestic economy and employ around one and a half million people. The sector is growing faster than, almost twice as fast as, the economy as a whole.'

Rt Hon Chris Smith MP, Secretary of State for
Culture, Media and Sport

The Nottingham Trent School of Art & Design

INTRODUCTION

'A challenging career that can be highly rewarding in both the creative and material senses of the word.'

Rodney Fitch

With over 2500 courses available in further and higher education, the United Kingdom is a world leader for career opportunities in art and design. Together with the USA, it is the most popular destination for overseas students wishing to study these subjects. No other country in the European Union has anywhere near such provision. The predominance of English as the international language of communication is undoubtedly an important factor, but the reputation of British universities as centres of innovation and creativity should not be underestimated.

For the potential student, the range of options within art and design is breathtaking, both in the breadth of possibilities and as a potential career. The creative industries are a burgeoning sector of the British economy.

An attractive aspect of embarking on a course in art and design is that the choices start broad and narrow down into specialist interests as skills, enthusiasms and opportunities develop. Most admissions tutors expect post A-level students to complete a diagnostic (a form of Foundation Studies) course, since they do not regard their background knowledge to be sufficient in the different branches of professional art and design.

This fundamental link between the thousands of jobs in art and design has a huge, but not always realised, impact on everyday life. One of the aims of pop artists like Andy Warhol was to show that objects we use without a second thought, like Coca Cola bottles, or tins of Heinz baked beans, are in fact, fine products of art and design. Whether it be the cars

1

we drive, the films, plays or television we watch, the household goods we use, or many of the other facets of life at the millennium, all are products of art and design.

It is difficult to imagine a world devoid of such creative impact, yet the image of the artist as an impoverished 'man apart' generally persists and contributes to the reluctance of some parents to encourage their offspring to seek careers in this area. Although such attitudes are well-intentioned, they are far off the mark in a time of rapid change when the idea of a 'job for life' is rapidly becoming a thing of the past. Increasingly, the emphasis is on the kind of sustainable and transferable skills that are the prerequisite for the wide range of careers in art and design. These qualities are both immediate and relevant. In the view of leading British designer, Rodney Fitch, 'it is definitely the business to be in, a challenging career that can be highly rewarding in both the creative and material senses of the word'.

The fact that the skills involved in art and design combine those ancient crafts that helped man to achieve his civilised identity like painting, drawing and carving, together with modern state-of-the-art computer skills and technology, is another factor that appeals greatly to Rodney Fitch. 'It is always changing, but this does mean that no one should go into it who is not prepared to be entirely flexible. Competition is fierce and getting fiercer, particularly for the recent graduate. If you're going to succeed, there'll be many occasions when you need to forget the nine-to-five mentality. Deadlines are the name of the game and the more successful you are, the tighter they become.'

Chapter 1
WHICH CAREER IN ART AND DESIGN?

Think of the objects in the family home, from chairs and tables to hi-fi equipment and microwave ovens; consider the amenities that we can visit, from libraries and shopping precincts to theme parks; and think of the computer games you play and the adverts on TV – all these things have been professionally designed. Ex-students of art and design schools are now influential in food packaging, fashion promotion, special effects, music videos, museum displays, car interiors, medical photography and jewellery design.

Art and design offers a huge range of specialisations and skills, increasingly including occupations requiring leading-edge technological skills. The common denominator linking these and thousands of other interesting jobs is that the standard training route will often require the development of art and design skills at higher education level. Even if your long-term plan is to become self-employed you will need to have mastered the skills of your trade and to have an understanding of marketing and business. Without the right education it will be difficult, although obviously not impossible, to achieve your career aspirations.

Art and design education ranges through more than 70 disciplines, from craft-orientated subjects like stained glass and tapestry to the fast-moving technology of computer graphics and multimedia. These may be broadly categorised under eight different headings: fine art; new media; graphic design; fashion and textile design; three-dimensional design; film, photography and video; history of art and design; arts and design management; although in many cases the lines between them are blurred, with skills and knowledge in one area impinging strongly on others. Most fine art courses, for example, include a strong element of art history

3

and the chance to explore a range of media. Increasingly, the boundaries between the old specialisations are being broken down by the advent of new media and study options reflect this.

FINE ART

In the popular mind, the terms 'art' and 'fine art' remain synonymous, evoking the traditional crafts of painting, drawing and sculpture. Such perceptions are the source of much parental disquiet about a career in the arts and, to some extent, these misgivings are well founded. Relatively few graduates in fine art are able to turn their talents into a full-time job. There is a clear analogy with acting in this. A small minority of drama students will find fame and fortune: a larger minority make a steady, but unspectacular, living. The majority, if they stay in the profession at all, sustain themselves with other jobs – *any jobs*!

Yet, just as there are people whose life's vocation is to act, so there are those who desire above all things to paint, draw or sculpt. And so it should be – imagine a world without art. The prospects are not entirely bleak. As well as the fortunate few who make the grade, fine arts graduates find opportunities in areas like arts administration, conservation, sale rooms and art therapy. Teaching is an attractive option for many – 10 per cent of fine art graduates teach. The personal skills that they have acquired such as practical and intellectual abilities, adaptability and flexibility frequently enable them to do well in other careers, often ones to which their artistic talents can make a contribution, such as in films, videos and publishing. Few find that their training does not have some sort of application.

An important component of fine arts courses is studio practice in painting, sculpture and printmaking. Increasingly, there are opportunities to work in the newer disciplines of performance art and digital media. Course content could include:

■ Drawing
■ Water- and oil-based painting of landscape, still life and the human figure

- Colour theory
- Assemblage
- Clay and wax modelling
- Arc and gas welding
- Plaster casting
- Art history
- Foundry and forge techniques
- Stone and wood carving
- Wood construction
- Lino and woodcut printing
- Intaglio and aquatint etching
- Lithography
- Silkscreen printing
- Photography
- Video and computer imagery.

CASE STUDY

Deli Nagel is 29 and a professional artist. She graduated from Exeter University with a degree in Fine Art and English.

'Fine art is becoming more and more entrepreneurial. There's a real place nowadays for the artist as businessman, trying every means to sell his product, manipulating the markets and bombarding galleries with mail shots.

'When most people leave college, they have to job it. Tony Blair bangs on about the brilliant arts scene in this country, but it's supported by the dole. I was on it, before I got a mad job chopping down trees. I went into the decorative arts for a bit as a way to make money. I started off painting people's walls and cupboards. It's a good way to show off a few skills. You get talked about at dinner parties. I also did lots of portraits of children. Parents seem to be particularly keen on paintings of their kids asleep, so that's what you give them. Back to business and market forces, I suppose.

'I didn't do a Foundation course to get into college. I'd done A-level Art at Marlborough College, which has a highly rated department, so I sneaked through that way. Nevertheless, I really feel I missed out. It's immensely worth doing in itself.

'You get pummelled around at college. You've got to be pretty malleable, giving the impression of exploring everything, or so confident that you're going to do your thing, whatever the odds, but most of us aren't like that.

A lot of people simply gave up and went into something else. They do it to toughen you up. They're really there to bamboozle you into knowing who you are, I suppose, so you come out with an idea of what you think and what you want to do.

'If you're really successful, the teachers push you forward. Their great aim is to get their star students on to an MA course. It may have its advantages, but it "colleges" you up a bit more. I don't know of anyone who did it who's doing any better as a result, although one or two went into academia.

'You've got to be self-assured because you can so easily be knocked down by criticism. If you wait for the world to come to you, you might well miss it, so, after a great deal of frustration, I hired a place and put on my own exhibition . . . invited lots of people. Someone suggested I put in a portfolio of my drawings as well as the paintings and it worked! It worked! I got a big joint exhibition in a London gallery.

'I'm doing well now. Can't keep up with the work, in fact. I've just landed a commission to do a corporate job for a leading fashion company, the Arcadia Group, so things are looking up.'

NEW MEDIA

We continue to see dramatic advances in technology and communications systems. The general term 'new media' is often used to describe these rapid developments. Recent influences that have a direct bearing on design education include the growth of multimedia applications, the increasing integration of the Internet as a viable multi-purpose communications system and business tool, web design, digital media and computer animation.

Nearly all art and design courses now include some form of training in new media and specialist art and design multimedia courses are becoming increasingly popular and more widely available as demand for trained employees grows.

Because the industry is changing constantly, new types of jobs are being created all the time. Typical multimedia design careers roles currently include:

- Multimedia producer
- Multimedia project manager

- Web designer
- Multimedia interface designer
- 2D animator for multimedia/web
- 3D animator for multimedia/web
- Sound specialist for multimedia
- Digital video producer/editor for multimedia
- Graphic artist/illustrator.

Salaries can be high in these areas but students will be expected to have a broad range of skills, self-motivation and staying power.

The skills needed to progress into these fields include computer literacy, basic mathematics and a good visual language, in other words, the ability to communicate an idea visually.

CASE STUDY

Gordon Chinn is 26. He graduated in Design and Technology from Ravensbourne College and is keen to extend his knowledge and experience of CAD (Computer-Aided Design) as his career progresses.

'I've had an interest in art and design for a long time. When I left school, I did a Foundation course, which extended my interest in CAD as did my degree course. My parents are both Chinese, born in Malaysia, so when I graduated, I thought I'd like to explore my roots. I got a job for two years working in a cyber café in Kuala Lumpur This was fantastic experience. It improved my Chinese. I suppose I'm able to converse with a good percentage of the world's population. It also extended my knowledge of CAD, which was very much part of the agenda. I worked quite a lot with the website team.

'On my return to England, I got a job with Microlight. They're major suppliers of bespoke lighting to the retail trade. Some of the biggest chains in the world are amongst their clients, for example Sears. I'm working in their design department, which obviously requires a lot of CAD expertise, in terms of simulations, for example. My Malaysian website experience has proved invaluable too.

'I'm leaving soon. I've got the travel bug again. This time it's China. When I get back I'd like to get into a job that has a strong emphasis on CAD in the world of graphics. That would extend my range. It would be a dream situation if I could use my knowledge of Chinese too.'

GRAPHIC DESIGN

Courses in graphic design prepare students for work in the communications industries, where verbal and visual expression conveys ideas and uses images to inform, promote and persuade. Initially at least, the majority of courses are broad-based in both creative and technical content. Students may elect to become general practitioners, or to specialise in subjects like typography, medical illustration, graphic communication, corporate identity, magazine design, television and video graphics, web design, point of sale (POS) and packaging surface design.

Hand skills are still important, but much design work is now created and manipulated via electronic systems, using desktop publishing and altering layouts on the computer screen.

Although finding a job in graphic design is a highly competitive business, there are more career opportunities in this area of design than any other – in places like design studios and consultancies, public relations and advertising agencies, in-house departments, or as freelance operators. This range of opportunity is reflected in the fact that there are more higher education places available in graphic design in the UK than there are in any other country in Europe.

Graphic design courses may include:

- **Advertising**, which covers campaign planning and presentation to sell products and publicise events and services through various outlets including the press, radio and television, posters, direct mail and selling, publishing, printing, audio-visual and multi-media production.
- **Typography**, which is the term used to describe the forms of printed lettering used in books, newspapers, journals, consumer products, invitations, business cards, etc.
- **Print technology**, computer systems to create text and image processes.
- **Information graphics**, includes the production of signs and notices to convey information in shops and stores, on highways, in airports, railway stations, museums and galleries, sports grounds, hospitals, etc. Increasingly, these are presented in electronic form.

- **Calligraphy**, which is also known as pen and brush lettering.
- **Letter carving**, which is a specialist technique used for craft printing.
- **Illustration**, which is used wherever a pictorial element is required to support the text in a variety of media, including books, newspapers, journals, commercial products, etc. Its most specialised element covers the use of technical and perspective drawing to explain the mechanisms of areas such as science, medicine and archaeology.
- **Web design**, which uses new and exciting software and techniques to create vibrant, interactive and functional websites and web-based advertising.

CASE STUDY

Helen Byford is 22. She was born in Manchester, but her family moved to Portugal, where her father had a job, when she was a baby. She was educated at the British School in Oporto and took a degree in Graphic Design at St Martin's College of Art. Her first job is with the leading firm of design consultants, Rodney Fitch.

'Of course I got interested in art at school, but the only thing we really did was drawing and painting. That's why doing a Foundation course was so valuable. It introduced me to all sorts of things that I'd only heard about. That's how I developed my enthusiasm for graphic design.

'I'm really lucky to have got into one of the leading design companies as my first job. Rodney Fitch is a great encourager of young talent and one learns a lot working in such a powerful team. Our main thrust is in the area of retail image. Some time ago, one of the Sunday magazines did a feature on the huge influence that Rodney Fitch has had in the average high street. It's true. Many of its images come out of this office or from Rodney's previous company.

'I'll stay here till I've grasped all that goes on. After that, I'm not sure. Obviously, it would be nice to extend my range into other areas of expertise and experience, but I've no immediate plans. I'm happy here for now.'

FASHION AND TEXTILE DESIGN

Courses in fashion and textile design prepare students for employment by providing a thorough grounding in craft skills such as pattern-making, grading, voile-making and garment construction, as well as conveying vital background knowledge in the history of costume. Some courses are orientated towards promotion and marketing and may include trend forecasting, buying and styling.

The fashion and textile industries are international. Leading centres include London, Paris, Milan, New York and Los Angeles. Some courses will include the opportunity to visit agencies in such places. Graduates often work in other countries to extend their experience. Understanding languages is therefore increasingly important and many colleges provide classes.

Obviously, an important facet of fashion and textile design is the need to anticipate (or even set) trends. This has led to a number of specialised jobs like colour predictors, style consultants and fashion forecasters. Other graduates who move beyond their specialisations may go into areas like fashion buying, quality control and retail management.

Many fashion and textile departments devote part of the first year to the opportunity to sample a wide range of skills before a decision is made on specialisation. Specialist options include women's, men's and children's wear, lingerie, millinery, accessories, theatrical costume design, light tailoring, sports wear, knitwear design, European fashion and fashion design with technology. Fashion communication courses provide a background of knowledge for those interested in going into fashion journalism, illustration or marketing.

Within fashion and textile design, there are a number of specialist fields.

Clothing technology courses normally concentrate on garment production and management. If they include design on the syllabus, they can provide useful preparation for work in mass-market design.

In **Textiles**, options include printed and woven designs, knitwear design and manufacture, embroidery and tapestry.

Applied design is a further area of specialisation. Options are available in interior textiles and floor coverings (carpets, wall coverings, laminated floorings and other surface decorations).

Other career opportunities exist in buying and merchandising, sales, marketing, PR, journalism, garment technology and product development.

Caroline Foy is 24. She did a Foundation course at Winchester School of Art and took a BA in European Fashion Design at the same college. She is now working with a fashion PR company.

'I didn't want to do just an Art degree when I left school, but something highly specific. That's why my Foundation course was so good. It introduced me to so many different aspects of the business. I hadn't intended to do fashion. It wasn't a conversion process, just a gradual dawning that this was for me.

'It was good to stay on at the same college to do my degree. I know most people have to go to their local college for their Foundation course, so I was lucky with mine, but I'd advise anyone who's looking into it all to take this possibility into account if there's a chance of it.

'The course was fantastic. I made my own collection, which is good career portfolio material, and you end up with a show.

'The course brought on my presentational skills fantastically. It all helps with my present job with Kim Blake PR, a leading light in the fashion world. I liaise with the press every single day, to try to promote stories and get lineage for our clients.

'The highlight has to be going to the big fashion shows, particularly Paris (they've not sent me to New York yet!). It's all OTT and quite pretentious, but a really good laugh. The people have that mixture of confidence and insecurity that everybody seems to have in what one might broadly call the arts world.

'The downside? I suppose that if you're in PR you have to be nice to everybody. It's also a bit steep to live in London, but that's the price you pay if you want to be where it's at.'

Opportunities with designer labels

'If you are determined to work for a designer label in the UK the potential is limited. There are perhaps 400 jobs in total. It is worth developing other skills that are in short supply: pattern-cutting, textile technology, production management and studio management. The shortage of skills in these areas is a persistent complaint, not only from designers but in all areas of the industry. There are also still opportunities overseas where British fashion skills are highly regarded.'

Source: Designer Fact File, A Guide to Setting up a Designer
Fashion Business, British Fashion Council 1997

THREE-DIMENSIONAL DESIGN

Three-dimensional designers work with a wide range of synthetic and natural materials, including plastics, wood, metal, ceramics and glass. Their work is often divided into two categories. **Product design** is industrially based and requires a sound knowledge of production techniques and user requirements, as well as the ability to analyse the strengths and weaknesses of existing models with a view to instituting improvements. The term **Design crafts**, as the name implies, refers to craftsmen who produce items from their own designs, in small quantities, using traditional methods in small studios or workshops.

Courses involving both of these categories require students to be skilled in freehand drawing and to be familiar with form, shape and content. The history of design is an important component in most courses, as is, increasingly, the concept of consumer awareness.

It is generally the method of production that differentiates the two categories. Such items as furniture, knitwear, jewellery, pottery, packaging and glassware can be produced by mass industrial processes or by highly skilled and painstaking effort.

Industrial 3D designers can work for manufacturers, consultancies or as freelancers. Their design work includes 'brown goods' such as electrical equipment or 'white goods' like kitchen appliances. Transport enthusiasts can specialise in areas like boat and car design.

3D design centres may specialise in a number of areas.

The UK is currently the only European country offering specific higher education courses in **packaging design**. The discipline incorporates the acquisition of graphic and communications skills to relay vital information on contents and instructions to the consumer or handler. CAD (computer aided design) is increasingly an important element. A variety of materials may be involved, including paper, board, metal, glass and plastic.

Model-making is a growth area with a crucial role in many design-related functions. Applications include work for architects, interior designers, client presentations and product and industrial designers.

Theatre design is another specialised area where work can only be produced on an individual basis. It is one of the most subtle aspects of the design world, since the role of the designer within the theatre – and its related crafts of film and television design – should never be paramount, but one in which vital support is given to other areas of creativity, such as acting and direction. It is a craft that is based firmly on the fundamental skills of creative drawing and model-making. The stage designer has to be thoroughly conversant with all aspects of theatrical production, including stagecraft, lighting, costume design, scenic painting and special effects. Each of these is, of course, a theatrical discipline in itself and may form the basis of an individual career.

Exhibition design is another individual and specialised area, which is based on a sensitive understanding of the design brief. It includes such jobs as the overall design of exhibitions and of individual stands, museum cases, window displays and stands for sales promotions. The exhibition designer is required to master the fundamentals of design in such areas as technical and freehand drawing, the use of colour, lettering, model-making and CAD. The creative use of natural and synthetic materials like wood, Perspex, glass, hardboard and textiles is also basic.

Interior design is concerned with the organisation of internal space to maximum effect for industrial, domestic, cultural, educational, medical, leisure, retail and other purposes. Like theatrical design, it is integrated into a number of other disciplines, including architecture, furniture design, decorative art and lighting design. An essential element of the training is the ability to work in a team.

A number of courses offer career opportunities in the fields of industrial production and individual craftwork. Most courses in **Jewellery and gold**

and silver smithing give the opportunity to learn industrial design and the methods of mass production manufacture (generally in less expensive materials), related to the costume jewellery and cutlery industries. Courses also cover individual craftwork, which gives the opportunity for one-off work in precious metals. Work is also undertaken in other materials including wood, bone, leather and found objects. Courses include engraving, theoretical and practical work with gems and semi-precious stones, metal technology, surface finishing and metalwork.

The field of **Ceramics** is very wide. Courses give the opportunity to learn the varied manifestations of working with clay, including industrial processes and applications and studio skills in pottery and decorative and form sculpture. Practical work includes kiln construction and firing, mould-making, the preparation of glazes, slip-casting and throwing on the wheel. The related craft of **Glassmaking** also has a wide range of techniques and applications. It is offered as a specialist course in a small number of colleges. Areas of study include glass-blowing, engraving, etching, cutting, design, glass sculpture, sand blasting and stained-glass techniques.

Furniture design also offers scope for work in industrial production and individual craftsmanship. Studies may include design and construction, the technology of materials, ergonomics, upholstery, the history of furniture design and manufacture, model-making and furniture crafts such as joinery, the use of hand and machine tools, carving, gilding, marquetry and turning.

CASE STUDY

Stage designer Liz Lander is 30. She took a degree in Biology from King's College, London, went into scenic art and then took a second degree in Stage Design. She now works in television.

'My background is quite contorted. Halfway through my course, I decided that Biology was not for me, although I knew it would be a waste not to complete it. I developed an interest in the college Dramatic Society, but even that was different. Whereas everyone else wanted to act, I was happy to potter around designing and painting. The smell of the greasepaint got into my blood!

'After graduation, I got a job in the workshops at the Palace Theatre in Watford. I was keen to learn all the tricks of the trade like scenic painting, prop-making, etc. The word job is a bit of an exaggeration. There was hardly ever any money to pay me. Whatever there was went into the sets.

'I really wanted to go into stage design, but there really isn't much of a route to it from scenic painting, which seems odd, since the two crafts used to be virtually one. I was lucky. Because I was by then a mature student, they gave me a reduced rate on the Stage Design course.

'I enjoyed the course, although it was quite theoretical. I suppose I missed getting covered in paint. It was good to look at concepts, things like script analysis, and present your own ideas. A lot of the lecturers were thoroughly in touch with the theatre. The Lighting tutor was excellent. The practical skills were good too: drawing, model-making, etc. Most people don't realise that even the most blockbusting set begins as a tiny model.

'I got on well with my fellow students. They thought that the theatre was about education and communication. I thought it was about entertainment (it's really about all three). I was keen to get somewhere like the RSC or the National. Most of them thought that fringe theatre was the place to be. Ironically that was where I ended up when I graduated. After a spell at that, I got into TV. I'm now designing small budget shows and art directing larger ones – I've done *EastEnders* and *Smack the Pony*.

'Stage design is hardly a growth industry, but it's endlessly varied. I'm currently working on a project to convert a double-decker bus to tour round the country!'

Working in crafts

- It is estimated that the crafts industries currently turn over around £400 million annually. The figure is more than double that of ten years ago, with a rise of 20 per cent in the number of crafts businesses over the same period.
- Estimates suggest there are 25,000 people working in crafts in the UK although wider definitions suggest a figure ten times larger.
- Contrary to received wisdom, large numbers of craftspeople work in urban areas, rather than in rural ones as is commonly assumed.
- Some 96 per cent of craft businesses are one- or two-person operations and more than three-quarters of people operate as sole traders.
- Working as sole traders, craftspeople experience the difficulties common to many small businesses . . . In addition, few craftspeople

earn an income commensurate with their extensive training, skills and the long hours that they work. The flexibility of self-employment and fulfilment gained from the creative process are seen as compensatory.

Source: *Creative Industries Mapping Document*,
Department for Culture, Media and Sport 1998

FILM, PHOTOGRAPHY AND VIDEO

British colleges and universities provide what is arguably the largest network of photography courses – both broad-based and specialist – in Europe. Career options include advertising, fashion and editorial photography, commercial and industrial photography, television, film and video, high street photography, lab work and medical photography. The industry has been revolutionised by the advent of new technology and the introduction of electronic imaging.

As well as the wide range of specialist courses, always popular choices with students, most art and design courses offer photography options. Photographic processes form an essential part of any specialist course, although the weight of emphasis between the technical and the creative can vary greatly. Moving image courses usually teach production, mixing, lighting and cinematography.

Careers in photography are varied and each specialist area is different in the way that it recruits, trains and pays its personnel. Advertising, fashion and newspaper photography are popular options and it may be difficult to find a career opening, whereas there may be shortages of trained photographers in other areas. Salaries can vary enormously – medical photographers, for example, are paid a rate for the job laid down in national guidelines, whereas advertising photographers are usually self-employed and negotiate a fee for each piece of work.

CASE STUDY

Paul Harris is 25. He did two different Foundation courses and then took a BA in Photography at the Surrey Institute of Art and Design. He is about to take up a position as a photographer with P&O Cruise Lines.

'I did Art A-level and that's what I wanted to do – be a painter. I did the highly rated Art Foundation course at Swindon College. That was really good news, because it was while there I discovered that my real bent was for photography, so I did a second course at Trowbridge College, which has a strong department.

'In fact, I found the Foundation courses better than my degree course, which never seemed to turn out as planned. Nevertheless, I did do some useful and creative project work there. I spent a lot of time working with fashion designers and there was plenty of opportunity to work outside. I had a lot of input into an art-based jewellery book. No money in it, but a great experience for someone still at college.

'I did my dissertation on Nick Knight, the fashion photographer. He is also big in pop star photography. I was able to meet him, but only briefly.

'A great influence was Jason Evans, who works under the name of "Travis". He's another fashion photographer and does a lot of advertising work. He taught part-time at my college, so it was great having that kind of contact between theory and practice.

'There wasn't too much around when I graduated, so I took a job as a chef in a hotel in Windsor – cooking's another interest. I suppose I'd settled into that and a career in photography seemed a distant prospect when, out of the blue, came a letter asking me if I was interested in working for P&O. It was funny how it came about. Just before I graduated I'd sent a "round-robin" letter and CV to a load of long-shot places, but without much response. Then 18 months later, P&O wrote!

'I'm determined to make the most of this piece of luck. I'll be travelling to the West Indies and the Med. I'm looking forward to it!'

HISTORY OF ART AND DESIGN

Arts history graduates find career openings in museum and gallery work, arts administration, exhibition organisation, conservation, publishing, journalism, teaching and art criticism. They also enter the same general career options open to all arts and humanities graduates.

Most of the older universities offer the History of Art as an honours degree, usually focusing on the history of fine arts, namely architecture, painting and sculpture in the Western tradition. It is mainly taught as a theoretical subject, although some universities and colleges encourage the taking of options that involve practical subjects. However, the former polytechnics that have achieved university status have widened the scope of the subject considerably to include design history, film, cinema, graphic communications and industrial architecture. These are particularly studied in their historical and social contexts. It is likely that the older institutions will extend their scope to include such options.

Many universities permit the study of the history of art and design as part of a joint honours degree, or as a minor option. All courses include study visits and some expect students to have a working knowledge of one or more foreign languages.

Conservation of paintings, drawings, prints, sculpture, paper, furniture, books, artefacts, photographs, textiles, craft objects, buildings and monuments is an area in which study of the history of art and design has great relevance. In order to undertake such work, it is clearly necessary to have extended one's range to include knowledge of scientific and practical processes and key practical skills. There are a number of postgraduate courses available to teach these capacities, as well as opportunities for in-house training in museums and galleries.

CASE STUDY

Pierre Elena is in his early 30s. He is currently teaching Design History at Swindon College, School of Art and Design.

'I didn't come to design history by the usual means. I trained as an industrial design engineer and decided that if you were going to understand the issues you had to have a grasp of design theory, so I did an M.Phil. at Central St Martin's – my area of case study was the fitted kitchen. Since then, I've taught at a variety of institutions, including most of the colleges of the London Institute.

'Design was big in the 1980s when I decided to go in for it. It was all design management in the 1990s. If I can see any trend at all now, it's towards design education. People in other spheres have long done their degrees and then enhanced them with a diploma course. It would be good if the same thing happened in design, so that you had more people working *with* design rather than *in* design, bringing it to whatever field they're in, making design more of a consumer commodity, if you like.'

ARTS AND DESIGN MANAGEMENT

Arts management

Having been historically something of a poor relation in the arts world, arts management has assumed an increasingly important role, particularly as demands for public accountability have increased. The arts manager has taken on much of the role of the old actor-manager or entrepreneurial proprietor, providing skills in fundraising and accountancy, marketing, legal issues, public relations and personnel management. The number of specialist courses and in-service training opportunities is growing.

It is this emphasis on administrative skills that enables arts managers to move to different areas of the arts with relative ease, whether it be festivals, theatre, opera, music, dance or the visual arts. Some arts management positions in the larger and most prestigious organisations, either venues or companies, are highly paid, with annual salaries of more than £100,000. Others can be with smaller organisations or in part-time or consultative positions. Many people starting out on this career gain invaluable experience by working in voluntary positions with local arts organisations.

CASE STUDY

Ruth Scarbrick is 23 and is working as an arts administrator with the Demarco European Arts Foundation – a major force in the arts world – in Edinburgh. She graduated with a Law degree from Queen Mary and Westfield College, London University.

'I grew up in Berwick-upon-Tweed, a highly picturesque, but somewhat dull place. I get tired of hearing the only two facts that anyone seems to know about the place: that because of some historic anomaly we're still at war with Russia and we're the only English team in the Scottish League. It was refreshing to go to London. I got a lot out of my course, but I never really wanted to go in for the law. You need a particular sort of mindset, which I don't think I've got. When I graduated I wanted to travel, so I got a job teaching English in China for a year with the British Council. That certainly expanded my horizons. After that I worked in a French ski resort for a bit. I loved the job, but there's no future in that. Arts management was a very appealing thought. I've long had a great interest in many art forms. One thing that my legal training has given me is an organisational discipline, as well as a knowledge of the workings of the law, which might come in useful. The Chinese experience brought out my resourcefulness and even the ski resort must have played its part in extending my people management skills.

'I've been lucky to get a job with Ricky Demarco. He's a phenomenon in Edinburgh. Everyone here seems to have heard of him. His track record is fantastic, from his famous *Macbeth* on an island in the Forth, to his introduction of East European theatre into this country, to his pioneering of links with legendary artists like Josef Beuys. A magazine recently described him as the "irresistible champion of not only Scottish art but any art with a genuine content. His feuds with the Scottish Arts Council and Edinburgh City Council have become legendary." I must add that I find him the ideal person to work for and with, always ready to explain, but one learns most simply by being around.

'I'm staying on till at least the Edinburgh Festival's over. After that, I suppose it makes sense to get a formal qualification, if only to learn all the disciplines. I'm happy in my chosen world.'

Design management

The increasing number of courses in design management are designed for those who have an interest in the creative arts and in management, but do not necessarily have the skills to pursue a career exclusively in design (although they might have). The key function is to combine administrative ability with an appreciation of the quality of design and its role and function.

The design manager might function within a design team, organising tenders for work and ensuring that they are completed as agreed. Many organisations now have their own design teams in which the design manager plays a crucial part in ensuring a consistent corporate identity.

CASE STUDY

Alison Fogg is 27 and graduated in Modern Languages from Leeds University. She is currently working as an account manager with a top London graphic design firm.

'I always wanted to do art and began it at school as a fourth A-level, but eventually gave it up because of the pressure of work. My parents thought that I should develop my linguistic talents, so I did a degree in French and Spanish. I got a lot out of that and things have worked out well for me. If they hadn't, I'd probably be blaming them for not encouraging me harder to do art!

'When I graduated I did a Teaching English as a Foreign Language (TEFL) qualification, but there didn't seem to be much future in that unless you owned a language school. I embarked on part-time courses at Chelsea and then asked a design company in my home town for some work experience. They refused at the time, but then called me up a few days later to offer me a day with them. The one day turned out to be a crafty interview and I got the job as project manager! I was with that company for the best part of a year before the pull to go back to London became too strong for me. I was lucky to get a job on my first application. I now see accounts through from beginning to end – and build a firm rapport with the client. I've even been able to pass on a bit of work that we couldn't do to my previous company, which I'm pleased about because I owe them a lot.

'My language degree has proved very useful. At present my company's up for a big job in Brussels, so, as a fluent French-speaker, they'll send me there if I get the job. I hope they do!'

OTHER AREAS

Some design careers fall outside the scope of art and design education. Most notable of these are architecture and engineering design. The reason for their non-inclusion is that, although as subjects they have much in common with a number of the career options discussed in this book, the route to qualify in them is highly specialised and does not come within the compass of starting on a broad base and narrowing down to specialisations. To become an architect, for example, it is necessary to do a three-year degree course, followed by a year's experience in an architects' practice, a further two years of the degree course, another year in practice and, finally, to pass the Royal Institute of British Architects professional practice exam. Suggested sources of further information on these topics are included in the reading list at the end of this book.

Number of designers working in industry

Discipline	1994	1999
Design and development engineers	81,500	87,800
Architects	35,600	37,000
Graphic designers and artists	103,200	113,700
Industrial designers	18,200	20,600
Clothing designers	9400	7000

Source: Design in Britain 2000, The Design Council

Chapter 2
WHICH ROUTE INTO ART AND DESIGN?

Before making a choice about a career in art and design, it is vital to acquire an informed view of how art and design courses can be used in the world of work, the career options open to you and the characteristics of particular kinds of creativity. If you are at school, you should talk to those teachers who can give you an appraisal of your abilities and suggest the best way forward. You can surf the net and visit the websites that most educational institutions now possess, or you can send off for prospectuses.

Higher education fairs are held in many parts of the country, usually in the spring or summer terms. Most schools take parties of pupils to them, but if nothing is being organised you can always go on your own. They are like big trade fairs with representatives from most higher education institutions taking a stand. They provide an opportunity to collect prospectuses and leaflets and you should be able to ask questions and get advice. It's worth making out a list of questions before you go. Often the stand on 'Applying for Art and Design' from the Universities and Colleges Admission Service (UCAS) will be present, and you will find this a very useful source of specialist information.

You can arrange to visit colleges offering the kind of courses that may interest you. They all hold regular open days when you can talk to tutors. Many colleges employ part-time and visiting staff who are rooted in the world of work, but who find it valuable to spend some of their time in an educational institution. Many of these people have built successful careers in their chosen fields and possess the experience and abilities that you are seeking to acquire, so it is worth examining how they might help you.

It is through this kind of link that students of art and design often find job opportunities.

Since art and design courses have a strong practical orientation, it is important to look around the facilities and consider how they would suit your objectives and how well you would adjust to them. Many courses involve processes and hardware that you may not have experienced before. Some are highly technical and designed with the needs of specific industries in mind. Others place greater emphasis on self-expression and the development of students' creative ideas.

Issues like studio charges should be examined. All courses will impose a charge for the materials that you use. The likely costs are rarely itemised in college promotional material, so it is in your interest to find them out. They will have a significant bearing on how successful you are going to be in avoiding additional debt.

The availability of computer resources, the library provision and the opportunities for European exchanges are all issues that it is quite legitimate to raise.

In addition, you should try to find out things like the normal rate of applicants to places. If it is a UCAS Route B institution, do they take many applicants who put them lower than first choice? How many written assignments do students have to complete? What are the opportunities for study visits?

You should also consider non-academic factors when choosing an institution. Remember you are choosing a town or city in which to base yourself for a considerable time. Research shows that students' performance can be adversely affected by accommodation and financial problems. On your visit, check some key factors:

■ Halls of residence? Some of the smaller specialist colleges of art are unlikely to match the number of beds available at universities.
■ Sharing a flat or a house? A popular option, but in some places hard to acquire at a reasonable price.
■ Digs? Not as common these days. One art college accommodation officer reports that 'Landladies in this town seem to think that art

students will clog up their sinks with paint or create an impromptu mural on the bedroom wall.'
■ At home? More and more students are entering higher education while still living at home, possibly undertaking a long round trip to college each day by public transport.
■ Living costs? These vary considerably around Britain. London and the Home Counties are much more expensive than south Wales, parts of the Midlands, the north of England, Northern Ireland and parts of urban Scotland.

It is useful to inquire what recent graduates are now doing and how easy it has been for them to find jobs. This may give you an indication of how the college is rated in the outside world. It is also valuable to talk to current students about their courses, but it is important to be aware that another person's experience may not provide the best route for you.

It is worth mentioning that many people in the art and design field are self-employed – at least at some stage in their careers. Some colleges recognise this and offer courses in simple practical accounting skills like bookkeeping. Most institutions are very aware of the reality of commercial employment and many offer professional practice programmes at higher education level. The programmes cover business practice, marketing, copyright and other elements of industrial practice.

Increasingly, courses include work placement experience, a vital preparation for a highly competitive job market. Often the college will organise this as part of the curriculum. It is equally valuable to arrange a spell of work placement experience before you go to college. However, even if you do have the contacts to make an approach, you may get a negative response, since sheer pressure of work may inhibit the company from giving you a worthwhile experience. Ironically, such studios are often the best places to be in, giving real insights into the pressures, frustrations, opportunities and rewards of the job. Offer to do any menial tasks unpaid: make the tea, frank the post, or sweep the floor. It will certainly be worth it!

This chart summarises the usual routes into higher education courses in art and design.

ROUTES AFTER GCSE

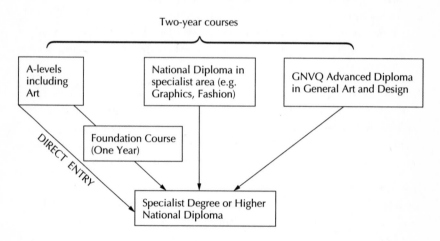

Most higher education courses in art and design expect applicants to have completed a Foundation course, a GNVQ Advanced course, or a National Diploma course in a related subject. Only around 10 per cent of students join through the direct entry route.

Chapter 3
FOUNDATION STUDIES

HOW TO APPLY

Fewer than 10 per cent of art and design places in higher education are achieved through 'direct entry'. The head of a popular fine art department, which admits 80 students each year, comments that in his ten-year involvement with his course, of 'the 800 students who have successfully convinced me at interview that they are worthy of a place . . . only five have come direct from A-levels.'

Foundation Studies represent the most common route for aspiring students of art and design into higher education. They ease the transition from school to higher education, forming a link between the type of work done for GCSE and A-level and more specialised courses. Most foundation courses last for one year, but in some colleges it is possible for students wishing to do Foundation Studies to join the second year of the two-year General National Vocational Qualification (GNVQ) course, which fulfils the same purpose while tending to be more work-related.

A list of schools and colleges running GNVQs administered by the Business and Technology Education Council (BTEC) is available from the Edexcel Foundation. See Useful addresses at the back. There are over 200 colleges nationwide offering Foundation Studies courses, so few students will live in an area with no access to one.

From September 2000 there will be a BTEC National Diploma in Art and Design, a two-year course that can be entered at 16. It prepares the way towards BTEC HNDs and meets entry requirements for many related degree courses. This new National Diploma will replace the present General Art and Design National Diplomas.

By far the most important entry qualifications for a Foundation Studies course are aptitude and commitment. Tutors will want to see samples of work done outside and beyond the exam syllabus, plus sketchbooks and notes and will ask about art-related interests, 'Do you watch art programmes on television or visit galleries and exhibitions?' for example. Much of the advice on portfolios on pp. 43–50 and 52–53 also applies to Foundation Studies applications. Course tutors receive more applications than places and can be selective.

It's also important to check what should go into the portfolio. Some Foundation Studies tutors, like their colleagues in higher education, specify the contents and the number of pieces.

Most students do not get a free choice of college. Foundation Studies counts as a non-advanced course, which is run by local education authorities (LEAs), which may use discretion in awarding grants and paying tuition fees. Most insist that their students attend a local college. Thus, unless students are prepared to pay for themselves, they are obliged to apply to the college stipulated by the LEA.

There is no national system of standard application forms and closing dates as there is for advanced courses. Each college decides on its own procedures. In urban areas, a number of colleges have grouped together to form their own mini clearing houses, so the applicant is asked to choose a selected number of them, but only has to make one application. There is usually a 'pool' system that allows students who are unsuccessful with their first choices to be considered by any of the others that have vacant places.

Whatever the system, it is up to the applicant to obtain the forms and to return them, although school art departments may have a supply. Not many colleges fix closing dates, but since places fill up and there are waiting lists on many courses, it is obviously important to return the forms as soon as possible.

WHAT DOES A FOUNDATION STUDIES COURSE CONSIST OF?

A Foundation Studies course helps students to decide which aspects of art and design best suit their talents and interests. It is also a preparatory course that helps to develop the skills required to gain entry to a higher-level course.

Foundation courses are very hard work. 'Nine-to-five, five days a week, with extra work at weekends,' says one course tutor. The period between starting the course and making higher education applications is fairly short, so it's pretty intensive.

Studies are divided into three stages. Although courses have a similar content, they are not all organised in the same way. The introductory stage is a broad course, which develops students' drawing skills, introduces them to a range of options within the main areas of fine art, graphics, fashion and 3D design and allows them to work in media they may not have tried before, like print, plaster, wood, metal, or ceramics.

In the diagnostic stage, students' work gradually becomes more specialised as, with guidance from their tutors, they begin to choose their final specialisation. Some courses allocate periods of time to different disciplines, perhaps a week spent on graphics, followed by weeks on fine art, fashion, photography and so on. Others prefer to cover several subjects at once. There are even some colleges that divide students very early into sets based on their specialisations. Whatever the course options, it is during this stage that portfolios are prepared.

In the final confirmatory stage, students complete their portfolios, study one topic in depth and start work on a major project.

Foundation Studies courses also include art history, critical studies and an introduction to information technology. Many colleges run optional study visits to European countries; Amsterdam and Paris are popular destinations.

ASSESSMENT

Students' work is assessed by a range of methods, which can include assignments, projects and practical exercises. A typical assignment for students in the diagnostic stage who were developing an interest in graphic design might be to work in small groups to produce a cover for a magazine. They would be expected to use several different skills: library research, drawing, typography, print, photography and, perhaps, CAD.

IS IT POSSIBLE TO MISS OUT THE FOUNDATION STUDIES COURSE?

In theory, yes. Universities and colleges may admit students through 'direct entry'. Those with standard higher diploma or degree course entry qualifications (i.e. a minimum of one or two A-levels respectively) may apply. Admissions tutors, however, tend to choose their students largely on the basis of a specialised portfolio and evidence of commitment to that branch of art or design. Some school pupils do manage to produce a portfolio, but they are rare. The A-level course simply doesn't give time to put together a portfolio with pieces of graphic design, 3D design and fashion, and so forth.

Chapter 4
APPLYING THROUGH UCAS

Most higher education institutions with courses in art and design expect applicants to have completed either a Foundation Studies course, a GNVQ Advanced course in General Art and Design, or a National Diploma course. A limited number of courses will consider applicants with A-levels only, but no more than 10 per cent of successful applicants gained places through this direct entry route. Entry requirements are listed in the specialist Universities and Colleges Admissions Service (UCAS) Art and Design handbook.

Applications for almost all art and design higher education courses are made through UCAS. It is worth consulting its publication: *University and College Entrance (UCE) – The Official Guide.*

Design courses within the UCAS scheme recruit through one of two equal pathways, **Route A** and **Route B**. Although there is no precise definition, the former route tends to lead to the more theoretical courses; the latter to take into consideration the special circumstance of students needing to present portfolios, etc. You can apply for a maximum of six places either through one route or spread between the two routes.

With Route A, the annual application deadline is 15th December. You can apply for up to six higher education institutions with no order of preference. Decisions on these applications are due not later than the end of the following April and replies to the offers will be required by the end of May.

Route B application forms can be obtained by ticking a box on the main UCAS form. They should be submitted between January and March in the year of entry. The big differences are that choices are listed in order of interview preference and that a maximum of three choices can be listed.

Interviews are conducted sequentially as listed. The first round is in early April, the second in mid-May and the third in mid-June.

How you wish to spread your choices is entirely up to you. It is likely that many art foundation students will want to take advantage of the extra time for portfolio preparation given in Route B. They can, of course, top up their application by listing three Route A courses to give themselves the maximum of six. It is possible to approach some courses through either route, but applicants are advised not to do both. It creates confusion. Applicants are advised to contact the college or university concerned if they are in any doubt about their preferred route.

Entry to the four largest Scottish arts institutions – Duncan of Jordanstone College of Art (University of Dundee), Edinburgh College of Art, Glasgow School of Art and Gray's School of Art, Robert Gordon University – is by direct application. Forms are available from November onwards. You are allowed two choices and the form must be returned to your first-choice college. If you are unsuccessful, the form is sent to your second choice and then, if necessary, on to the other two universities in the scheme. Other institutions in Scotland can be applied to through UCAS.

OVERSEAS STUDENTS

If you are a making an application from outside the UK you will fill in exactly the same forms as UK students. You may have to write first to UCAS to obtain them, however. UCAS sends supplies of forms to some overseas schools. You may also be able to obtain them from your nearest British Council office. Application forms for Foundation Studies will also have to be obtained individually. Forms have to be returned to UCAS except those from students from Cyprus, Guyana, India, Luxembourg, Tanzania and Thailand, which should be submitted through the country's student offices in London.

Many British universities and colleges, including some which offer Foundation courses, send delegates to attend higher education fairs in several countries. If you can get to one of these, you will be able to get individual advice.

The obvious difficulty you have in making your choice of course and college is distance. It may not be possible to make a pre-application visit, but if you can it will be worth it. Knowing you are here for only a short period of time, colleges should be helpful in fixing up appointments.

Some colleges may ask you to send your portfolio to them to be examined and may be prepared to accept you on that basis, plus your application form and references. Most, though, will ask you to attend an interview. This is something you need to check before you apply. Some colleges state that they cannot consider anyone who is unable to travel to the UK for interview. You obviously need to know which they are!

In order to decide whom to interview, some tutors ask overseas applicants to send a selection of transparencies showing their work and a letter of application. If they think the student would be suited to the course, an interview will be arranged. Most admissions tutors are perfectly happy to be flexible about interview dates and most say that they don't invite anyone to come from a long distance unless they are under serious consideration.

Coming to another country is a big step. Many universities and colleges have international student centres staffed by specialist advisers who are on hand to assist you. They also run welcome and orientation programmes, help students to find suitable accommodation and organise social events.

FILLING IN THE UCAS FORM

All admissions tutors want to see evidence that applicants are committed to their particular subjects. In art and design there are other important factors, which are bound up with the nature of the subject. In many other areas of higher education, the lecture theatre, seminar room and library are the main venues for college-based studies, but in art and design the majority of time is spent in shared studios with other students. To succeed in such an environment, it is important to give out the message that you are outgoing and that you will be receptive to the new ideas and interpretations that your fellow students will bring with them. It is quite legitimate to devote the larger part of Section 10 of the form to explaining why you want to take the course and how your interests and hobbies are relevant to this. You might include something like this:

- The part of your art and design course that you have enjoyed the most – and why

- Details of the project work you have done

- Possible aspirations and career plans

- A paragraph about any art, art history or design visits you may have made. For example, 'My art teacher recently organised a three-day visit to London. I was very impressed with the "Seeing Salvation" exhibition at the National Gallery. It brought home to me the commitment of artists and how it is perfectly natural to be influenced by the creative work of others, whether you are a famous artist or an A-level student. We also visited the National Portrait Gallery, the Hayward and the Tate, as well as some of the exclusive galleries around Bond Street. This gave me a fresh insight into the role of art in contemporary society and its function as a marketable commodity.'

- A description of the art work you do in your own time. A recent applicant listed snow-boarding as his hobby and went on to add that he had painted the design on his board.

OFFER-MAKING

The UCAS system works on the basis that the vast majority of applicants do not know the outcome of key exams or final course grades. In such cases, a **conditional** offer may be made. In many subjects, it is likely that this offer may be made on the basis of the application form and reference, but in art and design, it is highly likely that the offer will be made on the basis of inviting you (and your portfolio) to interview.

People who already possess the necessary qualifications may receive an **unconditional** offer. Obviously there will be few of these, if any, in art and design courses where the presentation of the portfolio is so important.

When you have had the final decisions from all your institutions you must choose between them. In fairness to other applicants, you are allowed to hold only two in Route A or across Routes A and B. If you have applied solely through Route B you can hold only one offer.

UNSUCCESSFUL APPLICATIONS

If a college or university has made you a conditional offer, then your results, when they are announced, will be make or break time. If you have not achieved the required results – the sad reality for thousands of applicants – then act quickly and positively. Telephone your first-choice college and enquire if they are still willing to consider you. Depending on the competition for places, they may consider a strong candidate who didn't quite get the grades requested. This could well be the case if your portfolio made a strong impression on them. If they say 'Yes', you breathe a long sigh of relief. You're in! If the response is 'No', repeat the exercise with your 'insurance' offer college, assuming that you have received more than one offer. If you are prepared to do it, you might ask them if they are willing to make you an offer for the following year on the basis of your existing grades. The admissions process is a very difficult one for universities and colleges, so they may take on someone who has known grades, particularly if you offer to do some course-related work during your year off.

If none of this does the trick, or if you have been unfortunate enough not to get any offers at all, your next port of call will be to participate in the UCAS Clearing System.

CLEARING

UCAS will automatically send unsuccessful applicants a Clearing Entry Form (CEF) with instructions before 1st September. You should not wait for the forms to arrive to start trying for a place. Lists of vacancies by subject area are published by the broadsheet newspapers from July onwards to enable direct application. They are also listed on the ECCTIS database and the Internet.

DEGREE COURSES

For prospective students, there are a number of degree options to consider.

Single honours

Around 20,000 places are available in art and design every year in British colleges and universities. Virtually all these courses receive large numbers of applicants. Some, particularly at colleges with worldwide reputations, are amongst the most competitive in the whole of British higher education. One subject, such as fine art, photography, furniture or textiles is studied in depth along with a compulsory element (usually one day a week) of history of art and design. This must be passed for the final degree to be awarded.

Combined degrees

A number of universities have degree programmes that offer art and design in combination with a subject, or subjects, from other academic disciplines, for example, Art and Psychology at Reading University. In addition, some institutions offer a mix of 'expressive arts' like dance, drama, music and the visual arts. Bath College of Higher Education, the Crewe campus of Manchester Metropolitan University and Nottingham Trent University are amongst those who provide such courses.

Modular degrees

Modular courses allow students to create their own study programmes according to their own needs, aptitudes and interests. This enables access to a wide range of subjects from different faculties and departments, so long as timetabling requirements do not create clashes. Such courses are particularly attractive to students with a wide range of interests. The Credit Accumulation and Transfer Scheme (CATS) allows students to complete a degree by adding together learning credits gained in different establishments. This means that it is becoming easier to study for a while, take a break and return when circumstances permit. The only problem is that there is no nationally recognised CATS scheme. You have to ask individual colleges and universities whether they operate it.

Sandwich degrees

In art and design, unlike many other subject areas, only a minority of degree courses have work experience built into the timetable. A 'thick sandwich' usually lasts four years: two at college or university, one year's employment and a final year back. In a 'thin sandwich', the work experience is spread in three- or six-month blocks throughout the four years.

DIPLOMA COURSES

Diploma of Higher Education (Dip HE)

This is a two-year course offered by some colleges and universities, usually with the option to progress, via another year's study, to a degree. The CATS means that credits from staged awards, like the Dip HE, are recognised by the majority of colleges and universities in the UK. Depending on the student's circumstances, it is possible to 'top up' a Dip HE into a degree, perhaps after a break of a few years from education, at another institution.

BTEC Higher National Diplomas (HNDs) and Certificates

BTEC's range of vocational courses are usually of two years' duration. A minority are offered as sandwich courses that take three years to complete. Courses are available in all the main design specifications.

The Scottish Qualifications Authority

The SQA organises vocational qualifications in Scotland and oversees a similar range of courses to BTEC in the main disciplines and associated studies.

OPPORTUNITIES FOR MATURE STUDENTS

'Mature applicants often undersell themselves. Their previous background and experience can be very useful. Often they don't believe that previous jobs are of any relevance. They are. Administrative experience qualifies a student well for the business context of interior design and will increase chances of employment after graduation.'

A tutor in interior design

Most universities and colleges welcome applications from mature students (usually defined as over 21). A lot of lecturers would secretly like to have their classes largely composed of them! Mature students bring with them commitment, motivation and an appetite for work. They have often made considerable financial sacrifices to return to study and are determined to make the most of the opportunity. All these factors easily outweigh any hesitancy or lack of confidence.

Many universities and colleges have special handbooks written for mature students, explaining what it will be like to return to study; how many mature students they have and whether any additional support is available in areas like study skills and essay-writing. If you are older than the average school-leaver and would like to apply for a course, don't be afraid to do so. Your application will be treated in exactly the same way except that institutions are able to treat you sympathetically if they so wish and relax the entry requirements. You can be accepted with lower or fewer qualifications than younger students.

Most institutions expect evidence of recent study though, and you'll need some help in putting a portfolio together. It's highly advisable to enrol on a local art course. If it's some time since you did any formal studying you might benefit from taking an academic subject. Remember that art and design courses are not just practical in content. They require you to present written work.

Your first port of call should be your nearest college of further education or adult education centre. They run courses leading to traditional examinations like A-levels and have courses exclusively for adults aiming at higher education. These are generally known as Access courses.

Access course

An Access course provides an opportunity for mature students who may not have the paper qualifications to enter higher education. As it is usually completed in one year, its attractions to the mature student over a traditional A-level or BTEC course are obvious. Colleges often run what are effectively pre-Access courses of the 'return to study' type for people who don't quite know what they wish to study or feel that they need to develop some study skills before embarking on Access proper.

Over 70 institutions – FE colleges, art schools and some universities – run part-time Foundation/Adult Access courses that prepare adult returners specifically for higher education in art and design. A list is given in *Creative Futures* (see Further reading). It is also worth enquiring locally.

Many higher education institutions operate Accreditation of Prior Learning (APL), which allows previous work or other relevant experience to be accepted in lieu of some academic qualifications. This is linked to the modular scheme CATS, which can provide another way forward for mature students.

It is also worth noting that an increasing number of degree courses are available on a part-time basis. The Open University is not the only example. It may be possible to begin part-time and negotiate a transfer to full-time attendance after a year or two. Applications for part-time study are made direct to institutions.

If you are a mature student who wishes for domestic reasons to live at home and will be applying to just one institution under the UCAS system, you are strongly advised to contact them and ask for an advisory interview with one of the admissions tutors. If you are only making one application, you don't want to waste it. It is more important than ever to visit, ask questions and in particular establish what kind of work you should be preparing for inclusion in your portfolio.

MONEY MATTERS

Further education

Grants are awarded by local education authorities (LEAs). Once you have been offered a conditional place on a course you should contact the LEA in your area to see if you are eligible for a grant.

Higher education

The main funding route is through the Students Loan Scheme, which you can apply to join through your LEA. A fee contribution may be payable.

Arrangements on loans and fees are subject to change and you need to find up-to-date information through your LEA or by contacting the Department for Education and Employment (DfEE), which publishes frequent guides on the subject. This information is also available on its website.

Currently full-time students starting courses of higher education may have to pay up to £1050 per year in tuition fees. These fees are means-tested: whether you have to pay anything at all or how much you have to pay depends on your family circumstances. For most UK and EU students loans are available to cover this cost. Your LEA will be able to advise you further.

You are advised to apply to your LEA for support towards fees even if you think you will have to pay the full contribution. If you do not apply you may be unable to receive student loans and grants towards your living costs. If you are a student from another EU Member State, you can apply for help with tuition fees but not living costs.

Students holding an award must produce evidence from an LEA, Local Unitary Authority, scholarship board or employer, confirming their responsibility to pay fees.

Chapter 5
WHERE TO APPLY FOR ART AND DESIGN COURSES

Thirty years ago institutions that had 'School' or 'College of Art' in their names were to be found in many towns and cities. Today, most art and design education is conducted in institutions that do not have these words in their titles. Absorption and incorporation have radically changed the picture. Henry Moore, one of the century's most influential sculptors, attended Leeds School of Art after the First World War. Fifty years later this was absorbed into Leeds Polytechnic, which has now become Leeds Metropolitan University. Nevertheless, although colleges of art and design have been absorbed into larger institutions, they have often retained much of their distinctive character and style.

Examples of specialist art and design institutions include Bournemouth and Poole College of Art and Design, Cumbria College of Art and Design, Falmouth School of Art, Glasgow School of Art, Herefordshire College of Art and Design, Kent Institute of Art and Design, Loughborough College of Art and Design, Ravensbourne College of Design and Communication, Surrey Institute of Art and Design, Wimbledon School of Art and Winchester School of Art.

The main providers of art and design higher education in Scotland are the Robert Gordon University in Aberdeen, Duncan of Jordanstone College of Art at the University of Dundee, Edinburgh College of Art and Glasgow School of Art. All run four-year degree courses. The first year is similar to a Foundation Studies year. Students taking A-levels or Highers apply for entry in the first year by obtaining a form direct from one of these institutions. It is possible to apply directly to start the degree course in the second year.

In 1992, over 30 polytechnics and colleges offering art and design courses acquired university status. Some of the larger multi-faculty universities incorporate large former regional colleges of art, for example, Belfast (The University of Ulster), Birmingham (University of Central England), Leicester (De Montfort University), Liverpool (John Moores University) and Manchester (Manchester Metropolitan University). Some former polytechnics have established art and design provision that has not been inherited from a former art college. Examples of these include Bournemouth University, Luton University and Teesside University.

In terms of numbers, the older universities account for less than 25 per cent of available places on fine art courses. Some of them have also incorporated schools of art. Two of the most prestigious are the Slade School at University College, London and the Ruskin School of Art at Oxford University.

Technological universities like Brunel, Loughborough and Salford mainly offer courses in industrial design and related disciplines.

The London Institute is the largest specialist art and design institution in Europe. Constituent colleges include Camberwell College of Arts, Central St Martins College of Art and Design, Chelsea College of Art and Design, London College of Fashion and the London College of Printing and the Distributive Trades.

Some colleges of higher education began as teacher training institutions and are still active in that role. They are, in effect, mini universities offering a diverse range of subjects in addition to art and design. Examples of those that incorporate a former college of art include Cheltenham and Gloucester College of Higher Education and Chichester Institute of Higher Education.

Sometimes very large in terms of student numbers, colleges of further and higher education can include a range of BTEC National and Higher National Diplomas, Foundation and degree art and design courses. At predominantly further education-orientated courses with only a handful of higher education courses, most students will be living at home. Examples of larger institutions include Blackpool and Fylde College and Stockport College of Further and Higher Education.

MAKING AN APPLICATION

The number of applications permitted to UCAS for degree and HND courses in any one year is a maximum of six. The limit for Foundation courses will be set by the number of available courses in your home area. In addition, it is possible to apply directly to a number of Scottish institutions which specialise in art and design.

THE IMPORTANCE OF THE PORTFOLIO

A portfolio is a folder containing representative samples of someone's art and design work. Artists and designers take theirs to job interviews or to show to agencies and consultancies where they are seeking commissions. Prospective students show their portfolios to admissions tutors.

The requirement to produce a portfolio is the linking factor between all courses in art and design. Its *quality* is the decisive factor in the offer of a place on a course. It doesn't matter how many exams you have passed, how much background reading you have done, or how many exhibitions you have attended, tutors need to see your work. Conversely, a good portfolio can make up for less than brilliant academic qualifications. Tutors will also want to interview you to assess your motivation. Many colleges invite applicants to bring their portfolios with them and to talk about them as part of the interview. Others expect to receive the portfolio in advance.

Most people have to prepare two portfolios: one for admission to a Foundation Course, the other when applying to a specialist advanced course. Although there are some common rules to observe, the two types of portfolio are bound to differ.

General rules to observe

■ Pick your best pieces for inclusion. This may seem obvious, but people aren't always the best judges of their own work. Follow your instincts but seek advice from your teachers.

- Don't include too much. Most colleges will send you advice on the contents of a portfolio.
- Be sure that you can discuss each piece of work: why you chose that topic; what you were trying to achieve; how you set about it.
- Include sketchpads and notebooks. Tutors want to see rough drawings. They want to see each stage of the work as it developed.
- Never pad the work out to make it look more extensive. This is obvious to the trained eye.
- Start and finish with a strong piece.

Preparing a portfolio for a design studies course

This should include as wide a variety of work as possible. You may want a career in fashion design, but you are applying for a diagnostic course whose aim is to enable you to confirm that or to point you in another direction. It's also intended to expand your range, so tutors want to see potential in all sorts of areas. Items selected could include:

- Drawings and paintings done from observation – figures, plants, buildings, landscapes, still life
- Colour work done in various media
- Charcoal sketches
- Pencil drawings
- Examples of design work and model-making
- Printmaking
- Photographs of three-dimensional work
- Photography.

Don't worry if you can't include all of these. Art college staff are well aware that schools and colleges have varying resources and curricula. What they are primarily looking for is *potential* and *motivation*, so it is very important that your folder is not limited to pieces of coursework. It should include samples of your own original work produced in your own time. This shows what interests you. It also demonstrates that you can do more than the minimum required without having to have an exam brief and away from the guiding hand of the art teacher.

You may also include a project, again with supporting notes and sketches, showing how you proceeded at each stage. If you have used art and design skills in completing a project in another subject, take that too.

Some colleges suggest that you keep a separate folder of work that has impressed you. It could include magazine illustrations, publicity leaflets, catalogues from exhibitions you have visited, prints and articles about designers. Tutors want to find out more about your interests and enthusiasms and may ask you about them at your interview.

Portfolios for specialist courses

Much of the above applies to these. Tutors are interested in your powers of observation, your ability to resolve problems, your wider interests and your all-round ability in art and design. They are also keen to see evidence of commitment to the area for which you are applying.

What follows are some suggestions of pieces to include when applying for certain courses. If you are trying for 'direct entry' and have no one to advise you, contact the various colleges (preferably by attending an Open Day) and ask what they like to see in a portfolio. If you are applying from a Foundation course, you will have your teachers to help you as well. If you are applying to a college that normally accepts students from your course, they will know very well what types of work usually impress.

Fashion – drawings; sketches; fashion designs; photographs or actual examples of garments you have made (to show pattern-cutting and sewing skill); a collection of information on particular designers, fashion manufacturers or shops.

Film, television and video – drawings, storyboards, scripts. You could enquire whether it's possible to include a short video that you have made.

Fine art – pieces of coursework, produced following a brief, with sketchbooks, working drawings and notes analysing and evaluating the outcome; original pieces, produced entirely from your own ideas, with notes as above; a collection of cuttings from magazines or brochures, with notes explaining why they interest you; work chosen from what you hope will be your specialisation, for example, paintings, or slides of sculpture.

Graphic design – lettering; freehand drawing; page layouts; advertising projects; publicity; packaging; typography; a complete publicity campaign for a product.

Illustration – work done from direct observation; work related to a design and technology product (if applying for technical or scientific illustration courses); work done to a brief, e.g. to illustrate a book, with sample text and notes explaining how you set out to emphasise particular aspects.

Industrial design – drawings, diagrams, computer-aided designs; working notes, showing that you understand manufacturing processes; preliminary sketches; photographs of the finished article.

Interior design – free drawing and painting using different media; observed drawing; work demonstrating application of colour in printing, collage, textiles, etc; three-dimensional projects in wood, ceramics or metal, showing problem-solving ability; sketchbooks and notebooks.

Photography – photographs with accompanying notes, explaining why and how you chose the subject and composed the picture. If you can develop and print your own work, do so, but colleges accept that not everyone has access to a darkroom.

SOME ADMISSION TUTORS' PREFERENCES

'I don't stipulate a minimum number of pieces or expect students to include an equal amount of different types of work. I am well aware that some schools concentrate on painting while others are stronger in decorative art or print-making, but it is essential that the portfolio contains drawings *from observation, not from photographs*. These can be landscape, figures or still life.

'From an A-level student I expect to see work done at different times over the two years, so I can see how it has developed.

If they have examples of three-dimensional work or textiles these can be included, as can work done for CDT or design and technology. These are all indicative of various strengths.

'There are two special pieces of work which other colleges may not ask for. We ask students to draw a full-length self-portrait and an environmental drawing based on the interior of a greenhouse or shed. This accustoms them to drawing in architectural space. They are always given three weeks to prepare these before coming to the interview.'

A Foundation Studies tutor

'We accept students from a variety of backgrounds and routes. Those applying from Foundation courses may not have had the opportunity or tutorial support to practise photography at a reasonable level. Those coming via National Diploma courses in Photography will be competent in the skills but their overall aesthetic sense may not be well developed. I therefore expect students from different backgrounds to include different types of work, but in all cases, I'm looking for evidence of potential.

'The portfolio can include all types of visual work and should always include support work – sketchbooks, contact sheets or any evidence that demonstrates the progression of ideas and how ideas have developed. Naturally, all portfolios must include photographs. I don't expect candidates to have developed and printed their own necessarily, since good processing facilities are not available to everyone. Images in black-and-white or colour, in print or transparency, should be included. We ask for a minimum of 12 pieces of work excluding supporting evidence, but do not specify subject matter. This is the applicants' choice. We do specify a need for an enthusiasm which expresses itself through the imagery.

A head of BA Photography

'Foundation courses educate students to explore and loosen up – a contrast to the disciplined drawings they did in schoolwork. I want to see examples of both. An art teacher will have, for

47

Getting into art and design

example, set up a still life to be painted over two or three weeks.
I can look at their objective, analytic drawing skill, assess their
perception and manipulative skills from such a piece and assess
their self-discipline, their staying power and their determination
to get it right. Drawings should always be included. They are
applicable to most areas of design, not, as students often
mistakenly think, to fine art alone.'

A course tutor for 3D Design

'In a portfolio we like to see work which demonstrates the
student's creativity and originality of thought. An understanding
of the design processes should be demonstrated by including
work sheets, ideas sheets, rough work or sketchbooks. We like to
see how the students think and develop their ideas. They should
also demonstrate an awareness and interest in letter forms, but at
this stage excitement about the use of typography is more
important than technical knowledge. We will also be looking for
evidence of sound drawing skills, colour sense and good
presentation of any finished pieces of work. In addition, we like
to see written work: a project or essay relating to historical and
cultural studies.'

A senior lecturer on a BA (Hons) course in
Graphic Communications

'We want to be able to see that they have understood a brief and
responded to it. They must also be self-motivated if they are to
have any chance of success. It is vital that they include work
done entirely from their own ideas. All applicants should include
sketchbooks, notebooks and any collections of material which are
evidence of their research, personal ideas and the kind of visual
phenomena they are interested in. We want to see what excites
them.'

A principal lecturer on a BA Hons Fine Arts course

AND WHAT NOT TO DO!

'I see vast portfolios containing everything but the kitchen sink and, in many cases, with little or no attempt at selection.'

'I suggest a maximum of 20 pieces – and no more than one piece of hand luggage at interview time – containing examples of three-dimensional work.'

'I don't have time to wade through pieces of work – some of which are put in upside down – looking for what the student is trying to tell me and then find explanatory notes 15 pages further on. Work should be presented in a logical sequence, with all the sketches, notes and explanations following each individual piece.'

'Personally, I am sceptical of the growing tendency to include scrapbooks and collections of other people's work unless it is done properly. There is nothing wrong with it, *but* students need to tell me why they have included particular cuttings, what interests them about the designer's work, what investigations they have carried out into his or her methods, why they approve of the materials used and so on. Obviously, both the scrapbook and the examples of original work should be relevant to the area that the student hopes to specialise in.'

TIPS

■ Presentation is important. Buy a portfolio – or make one. The portfolio itself can demonstrate your design skill. The pieces inside need not be expensively window mounted or contained in plastic covers, but they should be clearly and neatly labelled.

■ The portfolio should be large enough to hold all your work without any pieces being folded.

■ If you send it in advance, make sure that the portfolio is clearly labelled with your name and address and that every piece inside is signed and dated.

- You may enclose photographs of any three-dimensional work you wish the tutors to see and, provided that pieces are not too difficult to transport, take them with you to the interview.

- Get a portfolio with a shoulder strap. You'll find it useful as you slog to interviews by bus, train and foot.

Chapter 6
GETTING THE MOST FROM YOUR INTERVIEW

'The interview is not merely about selecting the best students for the course. It is imperative for us to know that, but it also helps the students to decide a college. They are interviewing us too! They need to know that they would be happy here.'

An admissions tutor

Interviews are generally nerve-racking things, although some people actually enjoy them! Admissions tutors are used to nervous people and will make allowances. They want to know more about you and to try and find out whether you are a suited to a career as a professional artist or designer. They also want to know if you are the right sort of person for their course. Art tutors and students spend much more time working closely together than those on most other higher education courses. It is important for staff to identify students who will fit in and jell together as a group.

PREPARATION

You will do so much better and be more confident if you spend time before each interview preparing for it, making sure that you are as up to date with your subject as possible through background reading and visits and can therefore express opinions if asked and can give clear reasons for your choice of course. You should be ready to answer questions about your present work and what you like or dislike about it. You can make intelligent guesses about other likely questions and go through some answers, but don't make them sound too pat and prepared.

It is important to re-read the prospectus and any other course information you may have before the interview. You may be asked what you know about the way in which the course is taught (the Open Day should come in useful here), or why you have applied to study at that particular centre. Remember that the tutors will have seen your application form which lists several other places. They are normally familiar with other departments in their field and are often interested in your reaction to them. They often like evidence of consistency, in other words, that you have used the same criteria in choosing all your courses.

It's a good idea to use your answers as an opportunity to give insights into your aspirations and motives. If you're asked why you applied for a particular course, it gives you the chance to explain why this aspect of art and design is for you – or why you are applying to do a diagnostic course first in the case of Foundation Studies applicants.

EXAMPLES OF QUESTIONS SPECIFIC TO ART AND DESIGN

The following list gives some typical general questions you might be asked at the interview:

- Discuss the work of a modern designer (sometimes you choose him or her, sometimes they choose).
- Discuss recent trends in production methods in graphic design.
- Discuss examples of contemporary three-dimensional design and comment on fashions in a particular period.
- Comment on two different paintings shown by the interviewer.
- Discuss your favourite medium.

THE ROLE OF THE PORTFOLIO

There is no rule about the number of people who may interview you. It may be just one, or two or three. By far the most common way for the interviewer(s) to begin is to ask you to talk about the contents of your portfolio. This has the advantage that you start by talking about something you know very well indeed. The interviewer(s) will ask you to describe why you did these pieces of work and the problems you had to overcome. He, she or they will then ask you more detailed questions – about the background research you undertook, the influences on your work and so on. Be ready to justify the work you have included in the portfolio. It has been known for a student to be asked, 'You are applying for a fine art course. Don't you think this work is more relevant to graphic design?'

SOME INTERVIEW TIPS

Your subject

■ Do as much background reading as you can. Go to the library and read art and design magazines.
■ Read a quality daily paper. They often contain articles about art, design and architecture.
■ Ask your art teacher or lecturer for advice. He or she will know the sort of questions previous applicants have been asked.
■ Try to organise a mock interview.

The interview itself

■ Get there early. Allow plenty of time.
■ Dress comfortably. You are not being interviewed for a job as a lawyer or accountant. Suits are not needed, but the tutors may like to feel that you've made an effort. Smart casual is probably the best. If you are a prospective fashion student you could wear something that you've designed or made. Don't wear anything that's going to make you feel restricted, uncomfortable or nervous. The idea is that you should forget about your appearance and concentrate on what you are saying.
■ Be patient. The waiting time and the interview itself may take longer than expected.
■ The golden rule is *never bluff*. If you don't understand a question or can't think of a reply, it's better to say so.

- Afterwards, analyse your answers and work out if you could have answered any questions better. It's good practice for next time.
- Don't expect an on-the-spot offer of a place. The interviewers have other people to see.

SOME ADVICE FROM TUTORS

'I ask what aspects of art they are enjoying at the moment and I always want to know whether they have any future career intentions. "No, I have only vague ideas and that's why I need to do a Foundation Studies course" is a perfectly valid answer. If, on the other hand, they seem locked into graphics, I ask whether they are prepared to give equal commitment to every part of the course. There are no options at all in the first term. Every student has to try everything.

'We see a batch of students, then make our decisions, There are two to three applicants for each place, so a lot are going to be disappointed. We do our best to suggest alternatives to unsuccessful candidates. This might mean, for example, suggesting an application to a specialist National Diploma course in graphics fashion.'

A course tutor in Foundation Studies

'Interviews normally involve myself or another experienced member of the department together with a student from the current Foundation year. We are looking for evidence of future potential rather than for any kind of past experience or knowledge. A Foundation course like ours is all about innovation and creative change, so we try hard not to have any preconceived templates that students are expected to fit. Ours is a very wide-ranging course leading to a staggering range of possible specialisations, so all sorts of interests could be relevant. My tendency is to say: "If in doubt, tell me about it."'

A head of Foundation Studies

'All applicants have a 30-minute interview with two members of staff. We try to make it as relaxed as possible. We want them to give their best, because we want the best students! We take the procedure very seriously; a successful selection process means a successful future for the programme.

'I always ask staff to interview in relation to the applicant's background. We have different criteria for accepting students from, for example, Foundation as against BTEC National Diploma courses.

'We usually view 2D portfolios without the student being present. This enables us to interview the applicant, not the portfolio! Those with show reels should remember that we do not want to see a 50-minute sequence in a 20-minute interview, no matter how good it is! Of course we are interested in the work, but our main interest is in the individual. What is their potential for the next two or three years? How well have they used the opportunities offered them so far? How do they relate to others? How well do they work in a group? What broader interests do they have?

'We like to know that students have visited us for an Open Day and are thus informed about the programme they are applying for. It's as much a case of them accepting us as it is of us accepting them!'

A subject leader in BA/HND Photomedia Production

'We always aim to invite all the applicants from one college to come on the same day. You soon begin to recognise "symptoms" of the course in their portfolios. Now I want to get to know them individually. We invite them to tell us about the aim of a particular project and whether they feel they accomplished it. Personally, I don't mind if they say, "I made a hash of this", as long as they continue with "because . . .".

'We ask questions about the field that interests them most, whether it be printmaking, painting or sculpture. This is because, somewhat unusually, we ask applicants to indicate which of three subject areas they wish to be based in and we have separate subject interviewing panels. Some other places do this, but most don't at this stage. I must stress that this is something that applicants should find out from the prospectus.

'We always ask which exhibitions they have visited and why certain artists' work impresses them. If they can't think of answers, it goes down like a lead balloon! We also expect to find evidence of interest in art history and in contemporary trends. Whether or not they approve of them is immaterial, but they should show some appreciation of what is happening in art at the millennium.'

A principal lecturer in Fine Art

'We organise the interviews so that students have an opportunity to find out as much about us and the course as possible. One of us talks to about 12 applicants for an hour, which gives them a chance to ask questions. While that's going on, two other members of staff are examining the portfolios. We like to make a team decision.

'Then each applicant has a one-to-one interview. I'm looking in particular for those who have an understanding of what graphic design involves. The content of the portfolio may be dictated somewhat by the course they are coming from. Foundation students may be very creative without having touched overmuch on design problems, whereas Diploma students may err the other way – be very good technically without having many original ideas. We can make allowances for this, but we must be able to see that they appreciate that graphic design is a problem-solving business and that designers have to satisfy the client's brief and not merely indulge their own creativity.

'I always ask what qualities they think they will bring to the course. One recent applicant looked at me blankly and said she didn't know. That showed a lack of preparation. She obviously had no idea of the requirement to be able to work as a member of a group.

'We also ask why they have applied to the HND course. The answers tell us whether they have done the research and found out what this course is all about.'

A senior lecturer in Graphic Communications

'Commercial art and design is a competitive professional field with graduates going into exhibition, retail, hotel and leisure design. The ability not only to sketch and model spatial ideas but also to communicate them is paramount. Candidates present their portfolios to us at interview. We like to see work in three dimensions – models in wood, ceramic, card and metal – and two dimensions, like life drawing, photography and painting. We look for flexibility of mind and the inclination to take risks with creative work. Extra skills could include knowledge of architectural history, experience of work in a design office and knowledge of computer-aided design.'

A course leader in Interior Design

'IT'S YOUR TURN TO ASK US'

You will probably want to know about the department's reputation. You want to know how you will be taught and whether you will like the atmosphere. Rather than saying, 'How good is your course?' you might ask:

- How many students normally use the studios at one time?
- Where do I buy supplies and equipment?
- How much might I expect to spend?
- How easy is it to get access to computers, libraries, darkrooms?
- Who are the visiting lecturers? (usually practising artists and designers)
- Have your students won any prizes and competitions recently?
- Would I have the opportunity to sell my work during the course?

Depending on the quality of the prospectus, some of this information may be given there. Check whether it is.

Never ask anything that you should already know from reading the information you have been sent.

Chapter 7
FINDING EMPLOYMENT

GETTING STARTED

With such a wide range of creative sectors it's not surprising that the routes to finding that first step on to the career ladder are very varied.

For some disciplines, self-employment is the most viable option and, once established, career development is a continuous and personal process (see Chapter 8). For the majority, however, at least in the first instance, a career means formal employment. And, despite the tremendous growth in the creative industries in recent years, getting work has not become any easier as more young people now go on to higher education and out on to the job market.

Increasingly, agencies and consultancies are looking for college-leavers who not only have creativity in abundance but who can quickly fit into often hectic working patterns and who come equipped with an awareness of marketing, business and self-management skills. A tall order, perhaps, but economic sense for busy entrepreneurs and business people who simply cannot justify long apprenticeships.

This competitive marketplace is generally recognised by the higher education institutions, which are increasingly liaising with industry to ensure that courses are relevant to commercial demands. In their last year most students receive help and advice in making contact with potential employers and developing job-hunting skills. Personal profiling, CV-writing and self-promotional skills are all included in this aspect of the course.

Employers are looking for a professional, positive and creative approach when sieving through, in some cases, hundreds of application letters.

Art and design students have a significant advantage over many other graduate disciplines in that they have a portfolio of work which they can use to impress potential employers at interview stage. Make sure your portfolio works for you.

WORK PLACEMENTS

Students are always encouraged to seek relevant work experience and, increasingly, agencies, design groups and colleges are setting up formal paid work placement programmes. This is a 'win-win' arrangement for all concerned. The college benefits from adding employment practice into the curriculum, the student gains valuable 'real work' experience and possibly a job, while the agencies get the opportunity to select the best candidates for further employment.

> 'It goes without saying that we are looking for creativity – that vital spark – and of course sound computer skills, but it is also important for a young designer to demonstrate a positive get-up-and-go attitude, an ability to communicate on a personal level and an awareness of marketing issues.
>
> 'Placements are a good way for us to judge potential employees – over a few weeks you can learn a lot about someone's potential – we don't expect fully fledged designers, just good raw material that we can help develop to their full potential!'
>
> *Director of a major London-based design group*

GETTING THERE

The key factors in ensuring relevant employment are determination, professionalism and flexibility.

Few young students will fall into a marvellous job at their first attempt but experience can lead you to where you want to be. Once in work it is vital to plan and manage your career path. There has always been a high staff turnover in the creative industries as people move on to improve their experience, skills and salaries. Knowing when to move and when to stay can be critical. Some agencies expect and encourage their junior staff to seek fresh opportunities and this helps to maintain a buoyant job market.

SOME TIPS FROM THE EXPERTS ON FINDING POSTGRADUATE EMPLOYMENT

'Try the specialist employment agencies for the fashion industry. Before an interview seek help from a professional or ask people already working in the industry. Find out what is expected from interviewees.

'There are various industry organisations that provide help. In fashion, the CAPIT B Trust publishes *Graduate Post*, where fashion and textile design students can advertise their skills to potential employers. There are industry or trade organisations for every creative sector and students should be aware of the ones that are relevant to them.

'You should also be aware of relevant trade press. The magazines for the fashion industry are *Fashion Weekly* and *Draper's Record*. These carry job advertisements.

'You can also write direct to companies but your letter will have to be good to get you noticed.'

A fashion designer

'Graduates will have to be prepared to take on any job they can get just to get on the first rung of the ladder. Vacancies tend to be for jobs like messengers or in office work. The pay is awful and the work can be boring but it gives you the chance to make some contacts and find out more about the industry. A lot of it depends on being in the right place at the right time and having the right skills.

'You can try writing direct to companies and keep an eye on the specialist magazines and the Media Guardian section of the *Guardian* newspaper every Monday.'

A lecturer in film and video

Chapter 8
SELF-EMPLOYMENT

In some branches of art and design, such as illustration, design crafts and fine art, self-employment is and always has been a practical necessity. Now too, the world of work is changing, becoming more flexible, and many designers move into a self-employed, freelance working role once they have achieved formal employment experience in their particular field.

Self-employment is not for everyone and certainly not for the faint-hearted. It requires determination to turn yourself into a one-person business, calling for marketing, selling, administration, accounts and time management skills as well as creativity. For some people, however, it brings the rewards of self-determination and financial independence.

Fortunately, as self-employment as a feature of the UK economy has increased, so have the sources of support for such workers. At college, professional practice programmes increasingly offer basic training in preparation for self-employment, while organisations like Business Link, banks and local Chambers of Commerce offer practical help in matters like developing a business plan and finding premises as well as in the critical issues of tax, VAT and national insurance.

For many small to medium-sized creative agencies, using a network of freelance specialist suppliers is the route to being able to take on a greater variety and volume of work. In fact, this flexible approach has long been a feature of the creative sectors, pioneering the way for its adoption by other commercial sectors.

Another positive development in this area has been the trend to combine formal PAYE employment with self-employment in various permutations.

Self-employment checklist

For	*Against*
You are your own boss.	Financial risk.
You make all the decisions.	Illness is not an option/ no sick pay.
You benefit from the rewards of your efforts.	No paid holidays.
Personal satisfaction.	Potentially long hours.
Flexible working patterns.	Work may fluctuate.
Variety.	Debts.
No office politics.	Isolation.

FURTHER READING

BOOKS

Choosing courses

Creative Futures: A Guide to Courses and Careers in Art, Craft and Design, National Society for Education in Art and Design, The Gatehouse, Corsham Court, Corsham SN13 0BZ.

Postgraduate Certificate in Education Courses in Art & Design, Graduate Teacher Training Registry, Rosehill, New Barn Lane, Cheltenham GL52 3LZ.

Questions & Answers Careers Book: Art & Design, Trotman & Co Ltd, 2 The Green, Richmond, Surrey TW9 1PL.

Questions & Answers Degree Book: Studying Art & Design, Trotman & Co Ltd.

UCAS/Trotman Complete Guides – Art and Design, Trotman & Co Ltd.

Finances

Sponsorship for Students, Hobson's Publishing, Bateman Street, Cambridge CB2 1LZ.

Students' Money Matters, Trotman and Co. Ltd.

Student Life: A Survival Guide, Hobson's Publishing.

General

Clearing the Way, Tony Higgins, Trotman & Co. Ltd.

Degree Course Offers, Brian Heap, Trotman & Co. Ltd.

Directory of Higher Education, Hobson's Publishing.

ERASMUS, The UK Guide, ISCO Publications, 12a–18a Princess Way, Camberley GU15 3SP.

How to Complete Your UCAS Form, Tony Higgins, Trotman & Co. Ltd.

Mature Student's Guide to HE, UCAS, Rosehill, New Barn Lane, Cheltenham GL52 3LZ.

Taking a Year Off, Val Butcher, Trotman & Co. Ltd.

University and College Entrance (UCE) – The Official Guide, UCAS.

Photography

Where to Study Photography, Film, Video and Television, published by The British Journal of Photography.

Working with Light, published by the British Institute of Professional Photography, Talbot House, Amwell End, Ware, Herts SG12 9HN. Tel: 01920 464011, also available on www.bipp.com.

MAGAZINES

Some of the key magazines and journals carrying industry news and features and, in many cases, job adverts. These may be available in school, college or local libraries. Alternatively, they can be ordered through newsagents.

Title	Published by
Advertising	
Campaign	Haymarket
Marketing	Haymarket
Marketing Week	Centaur Communications
Architecture	
The Architects' Journal	EMAP Construct
The Architectural Review	EMAP Construct
RIBA Journal	RIBA
Crafts	
Crafts	Craft Council
Design	
Design Week	Centaur Communications
Blueprint	EDP Ltd
Creative Review	Centaur Communications
Hotshoe International	Datateam Publishing Ltd
Fashion	
Drapers Record	EMAP Fashion
Fashion Weekly	EMAP Fashion
Film, video, television and radio	
Broadcast	EMAP Media
Screen International	EMAP Business
Sight and Sound	British Film Institute

Multimedia and software/digital media
Broadcast   EMAP Media

Publishing
The Bookseller   J. Whitaker & Sons Ltd
Press Gazette   Quantum Publishing Ltd

Visual Arts
Art Monthly   Britannia Art Publications
Artists and Illustrators Magazine The Artists and Illustrators
                                    Magazine Ltd
Art Review   Art Review Ltd
British Journal of Photography   Timothy Benn Publishing Ltd

USEFUL ADDRESSES

AN Publications – Artists Newsletter, PO Box 23, Sunderland SR4 6DG. Tel: 0191 514600

The Arts Council for Wales, Holst House, 9 Museum Place, Cardiff CF1 3NX. Tel: 029 2034 9711.

The Arts Council of England, 14 Great Peter Street, London SW1P 3NQ. Tel: 020 7333 0100. Website: www.artscouncil.org.uk

The Association of Illustrators, 1–5 Beehive Place, London SW9 7QR. Tel: 020 7733 9155. Website: www.aoi.co.uk

The British Film Institute, Education Department, 4th Floor, 21 Stephen Street, London W1P 2LN. Tel: 020 7957 8920. Website: www.bfi.org.uk

The British Institute of Professional Photography, Talbot House, Amwell End, Ware, Herts SG12 9HN. Tel: 01920 464011. Website: www.bipp.com

The Chartered Society of Designers, 32–38 Saffron Hill, London EC1N 8FH. Tel: 020 7831 9777.

The Crafts Council, 44a Pentonville Road, London N1 9BY. Tel: 020 7278 7700. Website: www.craftscouncil.org.uk

Department for Education and Employment, Sanctuary Buildings, Great Smith Street, London SW1P 3BT. Tel: 0870 0002288. Website: www.dfee.gov.uk

The Design Council, 34 Bow Street, London WC2E 7DL. Tel: 020 7420 5200.

EDEXCEL Foundation, Stewart House, 32 Russell Square, London WC1B 5DN. Tel: 020 7393 4500.

Graduate Teacher Training Registry, Rosehill, New Barn Lane, Cheltenham GL52 3LZ. Tel: 01242 544788.

National Society for Education in Art and Design, The Gatehouse, Corsham Court, Corsham SN13 0BZ. Tel: 01249 714825. Website: www.nsead.org

The Scottish Arts Council, 12 Manor Place, Edinburgh EH3 7OO. Tel: 0131 226 6051.

The Society of Designer Craftsmen, 24 Rivington Street, London EC2A 3DU. Tel: 020 7739 3663.

The Society of Typographical Designers, Chapelfields Cottage, Randwick, Stroud GL6 6HS. Tel: 01453 759311.

SKILL – National Bureau for Students with Disabilities, Chapter House, 18–20 Crucifix Lane, London SE1 3JW. Tel: 020 7450 0620. Website: www.Skill.org.uk

The Teacher Training Agency, Communications Centre, PO Box 3210, Chelmsford CM1 3WA. Tel: 01245 454454. Website: www.teach-tta.gov.uk

Textiles Institute, 10 Blackfriars Street, Manchester M3 5DR. Tel: 0161 834 8457.

UCAS, Rosehill, New Barn Lane, Cheltenham, GL52 3LZ. Tel: 01242 227788/444. Website: www.ucas.com